THE GOSPEL ACCORDING TO BARACK

Where Did Barack Obama Get His Ideas About Christianity?

Jefrey D. Breshears

Aréopagus
Publishing

www.TheAreopagus.org

THE GOSPEL ACCORDING TO

BARACK

Where Did Barack Obama Get His Ideas About Christianity?

On May 9, 2012 President Obama announced in an interview with ABC News that his views on same-sex marriage had "evolved" and that he now supports the idea. According to Obama, "I'd hesitated on gay marriage in part because I thought civil unions would be sufficient. And I was sensitive to the fact that for a lot of people the word 'marriage' was something that invokes very powerful traditions, religious beliefs, and so forth." (Note: It is interesting that when conservative politicians change their minds on an issue they are often accused of "flip-flopping," but when liberals do it, they are "evolving" – which if true, might be the best argument yet against the theory of evolution.)

The President's pronouncement was disappointing, but it certainly was not surprising to those who have followed his "evolution" over the years. But what was most alarming was that he cited his Christian faith to justify his position on same-sex marriage. As he put it:

> In the end the values that I care most deeply about and [my wife] cares most deeply about is [*sic*] how we treat other people. We are both practicing Christians, and... when we think about our faith, the thing at root that we think about is, not only Christ sacrificing himself on our behalf, but it's also the Golden Rule – treat others the way you would want to be treated.

Cultural liberals were ecstatic. Money poured into Obama's re-election campaign from his wealthy supporters in Hollywood. Larry Flynt, the infamous publisher of *Hustler* magazine, confessed that he had been "lukewarm" on Obama prior to this, but now he was "red-hot" in his admiration and zeal for the President and his agenda. (The thought of Larry Flynt being "red-hot" about anything is truly a chilling prospect.) And in a shameless attempt to boost sales for their troubled magazine, the editors of *Newsweek* featured Obama on their cover, crowned with a rainbow-colored halo, and hailed him "The First Gay President." (Apparently, this was intended as merely an honorary title – just as liberals lauded Bill Clinton years earlier as America's "First Black President.")

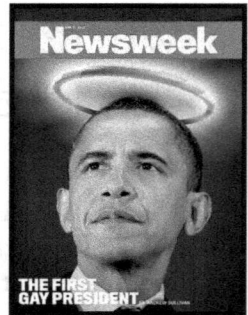

In fact, Obama had already done much to bring homosexuality into the mainstream of American public life. Early on in his administration he had repealed the military's "Don't ask, don't tell" policy that prohibited homosexuals from serving openly in the armed forces, and in 2011 he instructed the Justice Department *not* to defend DOMA (the Defense of Marriage Act) in court despite its being a federal law.

Obama's pronouncement was all the more strange given the fact that in 2004, as a Senate candidate, he had referenced his Christian faith as the primary reason for his *opposition* to same-sex marriage. At the time he declared...

> I'm a Christian, and so although I try not to have my religious beliefs dominate or determine my political views on this issue, I do believe that tradition and my religious beliefs say that marriage is something sanctified between a man and a woman.

Most Christians understand that Scripture is unambiguously clear that homosexual activity is sinful. Furthermore, Christian moral teaching has been consistent on this issue since the beginning. In fact, it was not even questioned until recent decades. Nevertheless, the question sometimes arises, "If homosexuality is wrong, why didn't Jesus directly address the issue?" – to which the simple answer is that homosexual behavior had always been regarded as sinful since the time of the Mosaic Law (ref. Leviticus 18:22 and 20:13) and was therefore not a salient moral issue in the Jewish culture of the first century in which Jesus lived. It was, however, a prominent practice in mainstream Greco-Roman culture, which is why Paul, the apostle to the Gentiles, alludes to it in passages such as Romans 1:26-27, I Corinthians 6:9-10, and I Timothy 1:9-10.

It is troubling that President Obama, a professing Christian, seems so bizarrely confused on a wide range of moral and religious issues. Throughout his political career he has been consistently pro-abortion, even to the point of opposing parental notification and supporting partial-birth abortions, a horrific and unconscionable practice. In 2008 he commented that if one of his daughters made a "mistake" and became pregnant, he would not want her "punished with a baby," and following the passage of the Patient Protection and Affordable Care Act of 2010 ("Obamacare") his administration announced that church-run institutions must provide access to contraceptives and abortifacients in health insurance plans for their employees. As Roman Catholic bishops later charged, the Obama administration poses the greatest threat to religious liberty in American history. Considering Obama's dogmatic stance on abortion, same-sex marriage and state-controlled religion, one is reminded of the prophet Isaiah's warning in Isaiah 5:20-21 – "Woe to those who call evil good and good evil! Woe to those who are wise in their own eyes and clever in their own sight." When it comes to fundamental moral issues such as these, woe to those who have the audacity to think they can redefine morality to suit their personal preferences or advance some socio-political agenda.

Thesis

My purpose in this essay is to reveal the roots of Obama's theology, which in turn informs and influences not only his social and political ideology but also his views on some of the most controversial moral and ethical issues of our day. This is strictly a theological assessment, and it is not intended to be either a personal or a political commentary. I do not know the President personally, and all I have are impressions of him based on his public actions, his public pronouncements and his public demeanor. His admirers consider him to be a sophisticated, eloquent and charismatic visionary, and at least on the surface he seems to be a loving and loyal husband and a good and attentive father. Conversely, his detractors regard him as an arrogant narcissist who is as corrupt and dishonest as any president in American history. It is worth noting, however, that we probably know less about his background and private life than of any previous president. In an age of information overload in which privacy is virtually a thing of the past, the fact that so much of his past is off-limits to public scrutiny is certainly cause for concern.

My thesis is simple. Barack Obama's understanding of the Christian faith has been influenced by two major factors: (1)Mainline Protestant liberal theology as mediated through the United Church of Christ; and (2)Black Liberation Theology as preached by his long-time pastor and mentor, Rev. Jeremiah Wright, in Trinity United Church of Christ in Chicago. Both of these influences are serious distortions of traditional biblical Christianity, and as such it calls into question whether Obama truly understands the nature of authentic orthodox Christianity.

Many conservative Christians seem certain that Obama is neither a true Christian nor even sincere about his faith. They contend that he is little more than a shrewd opportunist who has used his identification with Christianity over the years to advance his personal and political ambitions. The skeptics may be right when they assert that his faith is merely a facade, but it is also possible that he is indeed sincere but, like millions of other

Americans – including many who identify themselves as Christians – he is simply uninformed and confused when it comes to his understanding of the Christian faith. What we do know is that after he parted ways with Rev. Wright and Trinity United Church of Christ during the 2008 presidential campaign, and particularly since being elected president, Obama has rarely attended church even at Christmas and Easter. This is not exactly normative for most presidents, but nor is it unprecedented. Ronald Reagan, an icon to many evangelical Christians, was also a regular MIA when it came to church attendance during his years in the White House.

Barack Obama may or may not be sincere when he professes to be a Christian, but in either case his unwillingness to apply biblical standards of morality to contemporary issues is appalling and inexcusable. Just where he got the idea that biblical morality was subject to "evolution" is the subject of this essay as I delve into the origins and premises of mainline Protestant liberalism and Black Liberation Theology.

Mainline Protestant Liberalism: The Basic Tenets

As the charts on the following pages illustrate, there are fundamental (and irreconcilable) differences between the basic beliefs of theological conservatives and liberals when it comes to the seminal issues that define the Christian faith, including...

(1)The primary basis for doctrinal and moral authority;

(2)A philosophy of the Bible;

(3)The doctrine of the Trinity;

(4)The nature of Christ; and

(5)The essence of basic Christianity.

These charts are merely a general summary, of course, and it should be noted that there is considerable diversity among theological liberals when it comes to these and other doctrines of the faith. It is sensible that there would be more consensus among conservatives than liberals because the essence of conservatism is fidelity to the clear doctrinal and moral teachings of Scripture.

Theological Conservatism: A Brief Summary

Basis of Authority:
Special revelation as mediated through the Bible (as properly interpreted), and general revelation as mediated through God's creation and the moral truths inherent in natural law.

John Chrysostom: "A Christian is one who agrees with Holy Scripture, and he who does not agree with it has deviated from the one true faith."

Conservatives accept the core doctrines of the Christian faith as summarized in the early church creeds.

Philosophy of the Bible:
Divinely-inspired.

Historically reliable.

Doctrinally authoritative based on divinely-revealed truth.

Morally authoritative based on divinely-revealed moral absolutes.

The Bible has been accurately preserved and transmitted through the centuries.

If the Bible seems to contradict our current understanding of history or science, either (1)our biblical hermeneutic is incorrect, or (2)current historical or scientific theories are incorrect.

Doctrine of the Trinity:
God the Father, God the Son and God the Holy Spirit are three co-equal and co-eternal Persons who share a single divine nature.

Christology:
Jesus Christ is God incarnate and the spiritual Savior of humanity who died an atoning death on the cross for the sins of humanity and was raised from the dead.

Basic Christianity:
The essence of Christianity is the salvific mission of Jesus Christ who reconciles us to God and who is the sole Mediator between God and mankind.

Theological Liberalism: A Brief Summary

Basis of Authority:
Rationalism – Knowledge gained through the natural sciences, the social sciences, and human experience.

William Ellery Channing: "I am surer that my rational nature is from God than that any book is an expression of his will."

Liberals question or reject some (or many) core doctrines of the Christian faith such as the divine inspiration of Scripture, the Fall of man, the Virgin Birth, the Trinity, the Deity of Christ, the Atonement, the physical bodily Resurrection of Christ, etc.

Philosophy of the Bible:
An ancient religious text of purely human origins.

A mix of history, myth and legend.

There are no doctrinal absolutes; beliefs are purely subjective and relative.

Morality is relative, and the Bible contains some profound wisdom mixed with many outdated moral and social values.

The biblical text has been corrupted in the transmission process through the centuries.

If the Bible contradicts our current understanding of history or science, these disciplines are correct and the Bible is wrong.

Doctrine of the Trinity:
The traditional Christian doctrine of the Trinity is an irrational superstition.

Christology:
Jesus Christ, although merely a man, was a great rabbi, social prophet and spiritual leader who lived an exemplary life and taught some profound moral and ethical truths.

Basic Christianity:
The essence of Christianity is ethical humanitarianism based on the moral teachings of Jesus as encapsulated in the Golden Rule and the Sermon on the Mount.

Of course, conservative Christians often fall short in terms of living up to these tenets, but at least they acknowledge that these principles are absolute and that truth is not determined by personal preferences, social trends or majority opinion.

Among liberals, though, there is considerably more diversity due to the fact that liberal theology is intrinsically more subjective. Therefore, liberals are less inclined to accept and adhere to any set objective standard even if it is the clear teaching of Scripture. Like postmodernists, liberals aren't so concerned with what the Bible actually says as much as how it affects them personally – i.e., whether it seems sufficiently rational, loving, compassionate, humane, tolerant, etc. This allows ample latitude to pick and choose which doctrines, morals and ethical principles to accept and which to disregard as antiquated and irrelevant – such as, for example, the biblical condemnation of homosexual behavior.

Historical Origins of Liberal Christianity in America

In American history theological liberalism first surfaced during the Great Awakening, a series of revivals that swept through the colonies in the 1730s and '40s. The primary theme of the Great Awakening was the doctrine of the New Birth, which was not preached in most churches at the time. This was the central message of the great revivalists of the day such as Jonathan Edwards, George Whitefield, John Wesley, Gilbert Tennant, Isaac Backus and others, and the impact of the Great Awakening was considerable. During the seven-year period between 1735-42 an estimated 50,000 people experienced spiritual conversions, or about 3% of the total colonial population at the time.

Although popular in some areas, the revivals met stiff opposition from many of America's most prestigious ministers and churches. Some mainline pastors criticized the revivals on theological grounds while others were offended by the chaos and hyper-emotionalism that accompanied many of these events, and by the fact that some popular revivalists were obviously charlatans. Joseph Tracy, the first American historian of the Great Awakening who was generally sympathetic toward the movement, noted the social turbulence that accompanied these events:

> The whole land was full of angry controversy. Pastors were divided against pastors, churches against churches, and the members of the same church against each other.... The established rules of ecclesiastical order were [commonly violated].... Ignorant and headstrong men were roaming at large, pretending to be under the immediate guidance of the Holy Ghost, and slandering the best men in the land, and multitudes believed them. Religious meetings were often attended with disorders.... Conversions, most evidently spurious, were proclaimed as real.... It is no wonder that good, judicious, sober men were alarmed, that they pronounced the revival a source of more evil than good... [and] that they joined its opposers. [Joseph Tracy, *The Great Awakening* (Banner of Truth Trust, 1842, 1976), p. 433.]

Due to the emphasis on the doctrine of the New Birth, two controversies soon emerged: First, should churches restrict membership to only those who could provide a personal testimony of a spiritual conversion?, and second, should prospective pastors be required to provide a personal testimony of a conversion experience? For modern evangelicals this controversy seems almost unimaginable, but in American history the doctrine of the New Birth was the first wedge issue that divided theological conservatives and liberals.

Supporters of the revivals called themselves "New Light" Congregationalists or "New Side" Presbyterians, while opponents were "Old Lights" or "Old Sides." Among the influential critics of the revivals were Boston ministers such as Jonathan Mayhew and Charles Chauncey, but the foremost detractor was the Harvard divinity professor, Edward Wigglesworth (1693-1765), a theological liberal who taught for more than forty years and influenced an entire generation of New England Congregational pastors. Samuel Eliot Morison, the venerable Harvard historian who wrote the first comprehensive history of the institution in the 1960s, acknowledged the immense influence of Wigglesworth on subsequent New England theology:

> Wigglesworth... and his son, Edward, who succeeded him, had a very great influence on New England theology. It was the Wigglesworths who trained the pioneers of liberal Christianity in New England – the ministers who led the way out of the lush but fearsome jungles of Calvinism into the thin, clear light of Unitarianism. [Samuel Eliot Morison, *Three Centuries of Harvard, 1636-1926* (Belknap Press of Harvard University Press, 1964).]

An aside to this New Birth controversy is that churches that insisted upon a converted membership (and clergy) remained generally orthodox, while those that opened up membership to anyone and everyone drifted farther into liberalism and, in some cases, even Unitarianism.

By the early 1800s most of America's oldest churches and colleges had abandoned traditional Christian orthodoxy. For example, such was the case in 1808 when Andover Theological Seminary was founded by conservative Congregationalists in reaction to the Unitarian influence in Harvard Divinity School.

The Liberal Impetus

Why had theological liberalism gained so much ground at the expense of traditional orthodoxy by the turn of the 19th century? The origins of liberalism can be traced back to developments generations earlier, but there were at least five major contributing factors leading to the demise of Christian orthodoxy in both Europe and America.

(1)The legacy of the Reformation wars. Beginning in the 1520s Catholic and Protestant "Christians" intermittently slaughtered one other by the hundreds of thousands (and

Anabaptists and other dissenters by the tens of thousands) over the next 130 years. In Europe, the culmination of these religious conflicts was the Thirty Years' War of 1618-48, one of the most horrific wars in the continent's history. The war wreaked terrible death and devastation as marauding armies traipsed back and forth across Central and Western Europe, periodically pillaging the countryside and exterminating entire towns and villages in the process. As in most wars, disease and starvation killed off far more people than actual combat, but by the time it ended one-third of Germany's population had been wiped out along with large sections of France and other countries. Not since the barbarian invasions of the Western Roman Empire in the 5th century had Europe suffered on this scale.

As the historian David Goldman has written, "This was the definitive disaster in modern European history," and on a proportional scale the Thirty Years' War was even more destructive than World War II. And although the war was fought more for political than religious reasons, it contributed to the decline of European Christianity and the rise of secularism as much as any other single factor.

The English Civil War of 1642-51 had a similar impact. As with the Thirty Years War, this was primarily a political conflict in that it pitted the forces of royal absolutism against a Parliamentarian coalition determined to turn England into a constitutional monarchy. But religion was also a major factor as Presbyterians and Protestant Independents battled Anglicans and Catholics at the outset, only to have the alignments change in the second phase of the war as odd coalitions of Protestants, Catholics and Anglicans fought for supremacy.

By the time the nearly ten-year conflict ended, it was the bloodiest and most destructive war in English history. In England alone nearly 200,000 individuals perished (about 3.7% of the population), and Scotland suffered even more on a per capita basis as an estimated 60,000 were left dead, some 6% of the nation's population. But these figures pale by comparison to the death toll and the devastation that wracked Ireland, where over 600,000 souls (504,000 Catholics and 112,000 Protestants – 30% of the island's population) were slaughtered or starved to death.

[Note: To put these figures into perspective, the American Civil War was by far the most deadly conflict in U.S. history. During the four-year struggle some 620,000 American were killed in a nation of about 37 million – or roughly 1-1/2% of the population at the time. In World War II the percentage was even far smaller: out of a total population of 140 million, 420,000 Americans were killed in the war – a mere .3% (or 3 in 1,000).]

(2)The influence of the Scientific Revolution. The Scientific Revolution of the 16th century ushered in a new era in Western history – the "Modern Age." Amazing discoveries by Copernicus, Galileo, Kepler, Boyle, Newton and others enlarged humanity's understanding of the physical universe beyond all previous boundaries.

The key to discovering new knowledge was inductive reasoning gained empirically through human experience, experimentation and the rational interpretation of data. Significantly, it was *not* based on received authority – either tradition, superstition, mythology, divine revelation or Scripture. One consequence was that as science discovered natural causes for many of the mysteries of the physical world, it seemed to marginalize God as the direct agent behind these natural processes. By the mid-19th century, with the appearance of Darwinian evolutionary theory, God was replaced not only as the direct cause of natural phenomenon but as the indirect (or ultimate) cause as well – an assumption that went essentially unchallenged in scientific circles until the relatively recent advent of Intelligent Design theory.

(3)The influence of Enlightenment Rationalism. Beginning in the late 1600s some thinkers (*philosophes*), inspired by the remarkable new discoveries in science, argued that human reason should also be applied to the social sciences. This was the dawn of the Enlightenment, the acclaimed "Age of Reason," and

Enlightenment rationalism emphasized among other things the goodness of man and an evolutionary view of social progress. With Reason as our guide there was less reason for divine revelation – even within the realm of theology.

(4)Biblical criticism. Beginning in the Reformation Era, scholars began scouring libraries and monasteries in Europe and the Middle East, pursuing ancient texts in an attempt to produce new editions of the Bible that were as close to the original text as possible – the field of study known as biblical textual criticism.

In 1707 John Mill (1645-1707), an Oxford scholar, produced a new edition of the Greek New Testament that revolutionized biblical textual criticism. Over a thirty-year period Mill collected and accessed over a hundred Greek manuscripts, comparing their texts to the scripture commentaries by the early Church Fathers, and when he finally published his findings he cited some 30,000 variations in the texts. By all accounts Mill was a sincere Christian and an honest scholar, and his intention was certainly not to undermine people's faith and confidence in the Bible. But his research alarmed many Christian leaders who feared that his findings might be exploited by skeptics to challenge the divine inspiration of the Bible and the core doctrines of the faith.

Their concerns were confirmed just six years later when the English scholar Anthony Collins cited Mill's research to advance a deistic agenda. In his pamphlet, *Discourse on Free Thinking* (1713), Collins argued that the Bible was full of errors and therefore unreliable. The implications were sobering: if the Bible is so seriously flawed, if it is just a human book, and if we cannot even know what the authors originally wrote, then we are truly on our own and reason must be our guide – a contention that correlated perfectly with what deists were preaching at the time.

(5)The rise of Deism. Deism emerged from the Enlightenment emphasis on human reason. Sickened and embarrassed by all the religious-based bigotry and violence of the past, many regarded the Christian religion as a tool of oppressive political regimes. Certainly, history seemed to validate their contention: since the time of Constantine (r. 312-37 A.D.) institutionalized Christianity had often functioned as a support system for tyrannical monarchs. In addition, deism was a reaction to aspects of Christianity that many considered irrational. Justifiably so, deists objected to the overemphasis on ritual and doctrinal hair-splitting at the expense of ethics and social concerns.

Deism was an attempt to refine and update Christian theology using human reason alone and without recourse to the Bible. (As the Unitarian William Ellery Channing later expressed it, "I am surer that my rational nature is from God than that any book is an expression of his will.") In the process, a new concept of God and man emerged. According to the deists, God was the transcendent, eternal, infinite, and omnipotent Creator and Divine Architect of the universe, but he is *not* immanent, omni-present, or necessarily sovereign over his creation. Rejecting the traditional doctrine of the Trinity which they regarded as irrational, deists asserted that God is One both in essence and in personhood. As for Jesus Christ, he was a great moral teacher and an example of godly humanitarianism, but only a man. Most deists conceived of God as a personal Being, but others preferred to speak of God as an impersonal force or a unifying principle – i.e., "Providence."

Deists contended that all that can be known about God comes via human reason and General Revelation – i.e., knowledge gained from nature. Therefore, there was a strong strain of anti-supernaturalism embedded in deistic presuppositions. In contrast to biblical teaching, they conceived of the cosmos as a closed system and a kind of "clockwork universe" that runs like a giant machine according to fixed physical laws. This being the case, God is not actively involved in the world, nor can human beings have a personal relationship with him.

From this, it followed that any claims to Special Revelation – most particularly the Bible – were highly dubious. According to deists, divine intervention in human affairs is merely a projection of wishful thinking, and miracles, being a violation of the natural order, are simply legends and products of the human imagination. Deists equated supernaturalism with superstition, and saw no distinction between, for instance, the Roman Catholic doctrine of transubstantiation and the biblical doctrine of the Resurrection.

Deism also posited a new view of human nature. In their eyes, human beings are both good (or at least capable of being properly trained to be good) and rational (or at least capable of being properly educated to be rational). In contrast to biblical teaching, they contended that mankind's fundamental problem is not sin but ignorance and irrationality. Therefore, the solution to humanity's dilemma is not spiritual salvation but education and socio/political reforms that will liberate the innate goodness within man to be fully expressed.

Deism was popularized by the English Unitarian, Joseph Priestley (1733-1804), who brought the belief to America in 1794. In the early years, Unitarianism was quasi-Christian, and many Unitarians referred to themselves "liberal Christians." In their minds, they were simply updating Christianity to make it more compatible with modern thinking, and they certainly didn't consider themselves heretics. But their departure from traditional Christian theology began with their rejection of the doctrine of the Trinity, which they regarded as absurdly irrational. So rather than Trinitarian, they were "Unitarian" in their conception of God.

Embarrassed by the Christian doctrine of exclusivity – the belief that Christianity is the only true faith and salvation is available only through Jesus Christ – deists argued that human nature is basically good because human beings have been made in the image of a good and loving God. They regarded Jesus Christ as a great teacher, prophet, moralist and humanitarian, and some went so far as to even consider him some kind of demigod.

For decades, orthodox Christians and liberal deists contended for control of the most prestigious Congregational and Anglican churches and colleges. King's Chapel, the oldest Episcopal church in Boston and New England, became officially Unitarian in 1785, and by the early 1800s fourteen of Boston's sixteen oldest Congregational churches had become Unitarian. The movement was spreading all throughout New England, and many of these transitional churches included many of the most powerful and influential families in the region.

In 1805 Unitarianism became entrenched in Harvard's Divinity School when Henry Ware, an avowed Unitarian, was appointed professor of theology. (Three years after Ware's appointment, Andover Theological Seminary was founded by conservative Congregationalists as an alternative to the theological liberalism at Harvard.) From that point on Harvard became a bastion of Unitarianism, and the demise of traditional orthodox Christianity in New England was the inevitable result. By the second decade of the 19th century, few professors or students

Henry Ware (1764-1835)

at elite colleges professed belief in the core doctrines of biblical Christianity. So certain was Thomas Jefferson that Unitarianism would ultimately prevail that he predicted in 1822 that it would become the dominant religion in America.

[Note: In the 19th century many of the most prominent political and social leaders in Britain and America were Unitarians, including Joseph Priestley, Thomas Jefferson, John and Abigail Adams, William Ellery Channing, Ralph Waldo Emerson, Millard Fillmore, Florence Nightingale, Charles Dickens, Susan B. Anthony, and Samuel Taylor Coleridge.]

The United Church of Christ (UCC)

The definitive example of mainline Protestant liberalism is the United Church of Christ (not to be confused with the fundamentalist Churches of Christ.) Of the five denominations that constitute "mainline Protestantism" – the Evangelical Lutheran Church (ELCA), the Episcopal Church, the Presbyterian Church in the United States of America (PCUSA), the United Methodist church (UMC), and the United Church of Christ (UCC) – the UCC has been the most consistently liberal since its founding. In fact, the UCC is the most liberal Protestant denomination in all of American history.

The UCC was formed in 1957 in a merger between the Evangelical and Reformed Church and the Congregational Christian Churches, and at the outset the new denomination took as its motto John 17:21 – "That they may all be one." Theologically and ecclesiastically, the UCC describes itself as "Christian, Reformed, Congregational, and Evangelical" – but other than being undeniably congregational in church polity, many would question the Church's legitimacy as "Evangelical," theologically "Reformed," or even "Christian" in the traditional sense of the term.

In its early constitution and statement of faith, the UCC certainly sounded like a doctrinally orthodox denomination. For example, its 1961 constitution declared in part:

> The United Church of Christ acknowledges as its sole Head, Jesus Christ, Son of God and Savior. It acknowledges as kindred in Christ all who share in this confession. It looks to the Word of God in the Scriptures, and to the presence and power of the Holy Spirit, to prosper its creative and redemptive work in the world. It claims as its own the faith of the historic Church expressed in the ancient creeds and reclaimed in the basic insights of the Protestant Reformers....

> The Bible, though written in specific historical times
> and places, still speaks to us in our present condition.
> [Cited in Wikipedia: "United Church of Christ."]

The foregoing affirmations notwithstanding, the Devil, as the saying goes, is often in the details – or in this case, in the policies and programs that the UCC has sponsored and promoted over the past fifty years. Committed to ecumenism, the UCC is a member of the World Council of Churches and the National Council of Churches. It has an "ecumenical partnership" with another ultra-liberal denomination, the Christian Church (Disciples of Christ), and is in "full communion" with the Evangelical Lutheran Church, the Presbyterian Church in the USA, and the Reformed Church in America. The UCC is also integrally involved in various "interfaith" dialogues and cooperative efforts with Unitarians, Muslims and other religions.

Despite its orthodox rhetoric, from its founding the UCC has actively promoted a liberal/leftwing socio/political agenda. Although it prides itself in being "an extremely pluralistic and diverse denomination," in fact there is little room for theological or social conservatives within the denomination. In the forefront of most every liberal cause that surfaces, the UCC supports, for example, socialized medicine, open immigration and U.N.-sponsored "climate control" initiatives. Its "Tear Down the Wall" resolution of 2008 called on the Israeli government to remove the barrier separating Israel and the West Bank while ignoring the ongoing Palestinian rocket attacks on Israel.

In the late 1970s the UCC was the first Christian denomination to ordain practicing homosexual ministers, decades before the Episcopal Church or any other mainline Protestant denomination sanctioned gay and lesbian ministers. The UCC also "sanctifies" same-sex unions and affirms "abortion rights." In 2005, a resolution "In support of equal marriage rights for all people, regardless of gender" was supported by 80% of the delegates to its General Synod. In conjunction with the Unitarian/Universalist Association of

Congregations, the UCC has created a sex education curriculum for children and adolescents that provides "scientific and unbiased information regarding sexuality, birth control and condoms, and physical biology," including the free distribution of condoms.

In 2003 the UCC General Synod launched an advertising campaign entitled "God is Still Speaking." Apparently, if the UCC's positions on issues such as abortion and homosexuality are any indication, God's moral maturation is still in the process of evolving as well.

Some UCC congregations have resigned from the denomination in recent years, citing the Church's "theological surrender to the moral and spiritual confusion of contemporary culture" and the denomination's "often radically liberal political agenda." It is noteworthy that at the time of its founding, the UCC included about 7,000 churches and two million members. In the intervening 55 years, while the population of the United States has doubled, the UCC has lost nearly half its members and 25% of its congregations. Currently, the denomination's largest church is Trinity UCC in Chicago with an estimated 8,500 members, and Cathedral of Hope in Dallas, Texas, the largest predominantly LGBT (Lesbian, Gay, Bisexual & Transgender) church in the US with over 4,000 members.

Although a small denomination, the UCC has a long list of members who have been prominent public personalities including...

- Barry Lynn, Executive Director of the radical secular lobbying organization, Americans United for Separation of Church and State;
- Rev. Andrew Young, a civil rights leader and former congressman and mayor of Atlanta;
- Julian Bond, a former Georgia congressman and chair of the NAACP;
- Bill Moyers, former aide to President Lyndon Johnson and a PBS commentator;

- Rev. William Sloane Coffin (1924-2006), a notable UCC and Presbyterian minister, leftwing activist, and Senior Pastor of the Riverside Church in New York City from 1977-87, the flagship church of liberal Protestantism for much of the 20th century;
- Theologians Paul Tillich and the brothers Reinhold and Richard Niebuhr;
- Former Minnesota Senator Hubert H. Humphrey; and
- Former Vermont Governor and Democratic National Convention chairman Howard Dean.

Black Liberation Theology

In addition to mainline Protestant liberalism as mediated through the United Church of Christ, the other significant influence on Barack Obama's understanding of Christianity is Black Liberation Theology (BLT). Historically, BLT was the response by some black church leaders to generations of American Christianity that had sanctioned racism, racial bigotry and racial injustice. (Note: It was not until 1995 that the Southern Baptist Convention finally adopted a "Declaration of Repentance" for having supported slavery and sanctioning racial segregation for much of its history since its founding in 1845.)

An early version of Black Liberation Theology was put forth in the late 19th century by Henry McNeal Turner (1834-1915), a bishop in the African Methodist Episcopal Church. After the Civil War Turner worked in Georgia, serving the AME and campaining for civil rights. With the failure of Reconstruction he became increasingly militant, preaching a racialist version of Christianity based on the theme that "God is a Negro" – the point being that God identifies with those who are victims of abuse and injustice in this life.

Turner's theology attracted only a radical fringe of black church leaders, but in the turmoil of the 1960s there was renewed interest in formulating a specifically black theology just as the Ku Klux Klan had attempted to integrate Christianity and white racism. The modern Black Liberation Theology movement began in 1966 when an ad hoc group of 51 black pastors, calling themselves the National Committee of Negro Churchmen, bought a full-page ad in the *New York Times* to publish a "Black Power Statement." Rev. James Cone quickly emerged as the primary theoretician for BLT, and his book, *Black Theology and Black Power* (1969), essentially defined the movement.

Cone's career and associations over the years have exemplified many of the dominant themes in 20th century liberal Protestantism. Since 1977 he has served as the Charles Briggs Distinguished Professor of Systematic Theology at Union Theological Seminary in New York City. This is insightful in itself as Briggs was a high-profile liberal pastor and theologian in the late 19th century who was convicted

James Cone

on heresy charges in 1893 and suspended from the Presbyterian Church, whereupon he left the denomination and became an Episcopalian priest.

Cone's association with Union Theological Seminary is also noteworthy. For over a century UTS has been a bastion of liberal Protestantism, and a roster of its past and present faculty reads like a veritable Who's Who in American Christian socialism:

- Harry F. Ward (1873-1966), a Methodist minister and the first chairman of the ACLU from its founding in 1920 until the organization was pressured to expel all Communists from its leadership ranks in 1940;

- Harry Emerson Fosdick (1878-1969), an outspoken liberal apologist during the Fundamentalist/Modernist controversy in the 1920s who was investigated by the Presbyterian Church in 1923 on heresy charges, and who later pastored Riverside Church in New York City, perhaps the most prestigious and influential liberal Protestant church in America for several decades;

- Paul Tillich, one of the 20th century's most influential liberal theologians;
- Reinhold Niebuhr, one of the 20th century's most influential Neo-orthodox theologians; and
  - Cornel West, a professor of Religious Philosophy and Christian Studies at UTS, professor of African-American Studies at Princeton University, best-selling author, media personality, and the honorary chair of the Democratic Socialists of America.

For decades Union Theological Seminary was the prime institution where the American Communist Party referred its members who intended to prepare for ministry in mainline Protestant churches, and through the years it has produced more than its share of influential alumni, such as...

- Norman Thomas, a Presbyterian minister and six-time Socialist Party candidate for President of the U.S.;
- Myles Horton, founder of the leftwing Highlander Folk School in Monteagle, Tennessee;
- David Dellinger, one of the Chicago Seven terrorists who was convicted for organizing the riots at the 1968 Democratic National Convention in Chicago;
- Malcolm Boyd, an Episcopal priest, best-selling author, and the first prominent American clergyman to declare himself a practicing homosexual in the mid-1970s;
- Walter Bruggemann, a popular author and Old Testament theologian at Columbia Seminary in Atlanta; and
- Marcus Borg, a popular author and radical revisionist scholar associated with the infamous Jesus Seminar.

Although James Cone professes to be a Christian, he candidly concedes that he derived his theology as much from Malcolm X and the Black Power movement as from Christian theologians and thinkers such as Martin Luther King Jr. According to Cone, "Malcolm X was not far wrong when he called the white man 'the devil.'"

As with virtually any theology, philosophy or ideology, there are positive aspects of Black Liberation Theology – most significantly the social justice themes that permeate the Old and New Testaments. As the Declaration by the National Committee of Black Church Men, drafted in 1969, declared:

> Black theology is a theology of black liberation.... It is the affirmation of black humanity that emancipates black people from white racism, thus providing authentic freedom for both white and black people. [Quoted in Anthony Bradley, *Liberating Black Theology: The Bible and the Black Experience in America* (Crossway, 2010), p. 18.]

There is, of course, some truth in this sentiment. Historically, whenever true Christianity has been practiced it has always functioned as a force for humanitarianism, social justice and political reform. These are perennial Christian values that any understanding of wholistic discipleship must include.

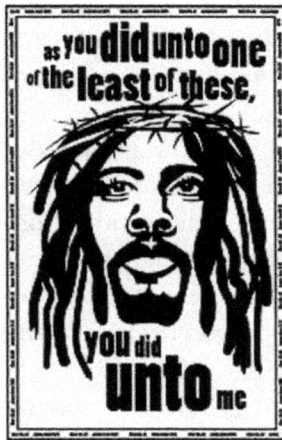

Another theme in Black Liberation Theology that merits mention is the deracialization of God. As Cone and his colleagues adamantly assert, God is not white, nor was Jesus a European. Since the dawn of recorded history, "white" or lightness has generally represented purity, virtue and goodness. In contrast, "black" has connoted darkness, sinister forces, and all things evil. The psychological impact of such metaphors on dark-skinned people could very well be far more significant than we imagine. White Christians are prone to dismiss this obvious observation as little more than racial pandering, but in reality there is value in challenging our casual metaphors and comfortable stereotypical images of God, a point that Cone has emphasized repeatedly:

> In reality, Christ was not white, not European. That's important to the psychic and to the spiritual consciousness of black people who live in a ghetto and in a white society in which their lord and savior looks just like people who victimize them. God is whatever color God needs to be in order to let people know they're not nobodies, they're somebodies. [Quoted in Wikipedia, "Black Liberation Theology."]

Unfortunately, the negative aspects of Black Liberation Theology far outweigh the positive, and there is a sinister side to this belief system that should alarm all serious Christians. The core of every Christian theological system is hermeneutics – the basic principles of sound biblical interpretation – and unorthodox hermeneutics is a fundamental flaw in BLT. For Cone, Scripture should be interpreted not according to its original historical and literary context but subjectively in keeping with the experience of black people in modern times (including, apparently, his own life experiences). For him, the essence of Christianity is a theology of liberation within the context of black oppression and exploitation. Jesus, who was an "African Jew," was first and foremost a radical social prophet and revolutionary who preached a Gospel of social justice and equality and whose mission it was to liberate all humanity from social, political, economic and religious subjugation. For this, he was criticized, harassed and eventually executed as a common criminal by the white power structure of his day.

A second fallacy of BLT is that rather than focusing on individual sin as the root cause of humanity's problems, it shifts the focus to social and institutional injustice. Therefore, the solution is not spiritual transformation and a renewed heart and mind but radical social change. The implication, as the 18th century *philosophe* Jean-Jacques Rousseau espoused, is that humanity is basically good but "society" corrupts – an enduring myth that is nonetheless logically absurd. Third, rather than emphasize forgiveness and healing for past wrongs, BLT tends to focus almost exclusively on retribution.

Fourth, and perhaps most insidiously, Black Liberation Theology is a volatile mix of two very toxic elements: (1)Racialism* and (2)Neo-Marxism. For Cone and other black liberationists, our core essence as human beings is our racial identity, and it is primarily through the prism of race that we process the issues of life. In fact, nothing could be more antithetical to the spirit of true Christianity than this obsessive fixation on race. In Galatians 3:26ff the apostle Paul writes, "You are all children of God through faith in Christ Jesus.... There is neither Jew nor Greek, slave nor free, male nor female, for you are all one in Christ Jesus." Had race been a major issue dividing his society at the time, I imagine that Paul would have inserted, "... neither Jew nor Greek, slave nor free, male nor female, *black nor white*, for you are all one in Christ Jesus."

In Black Liberation Theology, "white" represents a history of oppression, exploitation and imperialism – i.e., a culture of evil. "Black," on the other hand, represents victimhood – those who

---

* Racialism should be distinguished from racism, a much overused and misused term.

Racism is the belief that different races are innately (i.e., genetically) different in terms of their physical and mental capacities in that some are superior and others inferior. Racism is not the same as racial prejudice, bigotry and discrimination, although it is often a root cause of such attitudes and behavior.

Racialism, on the other hand, is an obsessive fixation on race to the extent that it primarily determines one's sense of self-identity and becomes one's paradigm for processing the personal, social, economic, political and religious issues of life.

While it is true that racists also tend to be racialists and many racialists may also be racists, the two terms and the beliefs they represent are not identical. And while racism will always be a problem in human affairs, racialism is actually a more pervasive and divisive problem in American society today.

have been (and still are) subject to oppression, exploitation and imperialism. According to Cone, "black" is not necessarily a condition of skin color. As he writes in *Black Theology and Black Power* (1969), "Being black means that your heart, your soul, your mind, and your body are where the dispossessed are." Therefore, at least theoretically, liberals such as Bill Clinton, Bill Maher and George Soros can be "black" while conservatives such as Clarence Thomas, Thomas Sowell and Condoleezza Rice are "white." But in reality, categories of black and white are almost inevitably tied to skin color.

A second incendiary element in Black Liberation Theology is Neo-Marxism, an ideology that interprets all the social and political issues of life through the Marxist matrix of dialectical materialism. Classical Marxism divided society into "good" and "bad" people along broad socio/economic lines. The "good" were the "productive" classes – i.e., the proletariat class of common laborers, factory workers, artisans, farmers and peasants who worked with their hands; the "bad" were the predatory exploiters – the bourgeoisie class of capitalists, bankers, industrialists, managers, landlords, clergy, etc. Contemporary Neo-Marxism perpetuates this kind of simplistic social stereotyping, except that now the "good" are the victimized minorities – feminist women, blacks, Hispanics, homosexuals, etc. – and the "bad" are white males, non-feminist white females, Christians and conservatives in general.

The division of humanity along broad sociological lines rather than according to individual character has been a recurring theme since ancient times, but it usually has been cast in economic terms of the rich against the poor or in political terms as the governing class versus disenfranchised subjects. Like sexual politics, racial politics is a uniquely 20th century concept, and Black Liberation Theology expropriated the idea to formulate a unique racialist and Neo-Marxist Christian synthesis. Just as classical Marxism separated society into capitalist oppressors and the oppressed working classes, BLT divides humanity along the lines of white oppressors and black victims. So in effect, God is not only "black" but also "red." In *A Black Theology of Liberation* (1970), Cone frames the argument accordingly:

> The black theologian must reject any conception of God which stifles black self determination by picturing God as a God of all peoples. Either God is identified with the oppressed to the point that their experiences becomes God's experience, or God is a God of racism.... The blackness of God means that God has made the oppressed condition God's own condition. This is the essence of the Biblical revelation. [James Cone, *A Black Theology of Liberation* (1970), pp. 63-64.]

For Cone, God's primary concern is for social, economic and political justice for the poor and the socially marginalized. As he puts it, "In Christ, God enters human affairs and takes sides with the oppressed. Their suffering becomes his; their despair, divine despair." In typically Neo-Marxist terms, Jonathan Walton, a professor of African-American Religions at Harvard Divinity School, explains Cone's colorized theology as an attempt to draw a sharp distinction between humanity's violators and victims:

> James Cone believed that the New Testament revealed Jesus as one who identified with those suffering under oppression, the socially marginalized and the cultural outcasts. And since the socially constructed categories of race in America (i.e., whiteness and blackness) had come to culturally signify dominance (whiteness) and oppression (blackness), from a theological perspective Cone argued that Jesus reveals himself as black in order to disrupt and dismantle white oppression. [Quoted in Wikipedia, "Black Liberation Theology."]

A general underlying theme in the theological ideology of the Christian Left is that "God is on the side of the poor." Indisputably, God is a God of social justice, and as such God hates all sin – including the unwarranted marginalization, exploitation and oppression of any individual or group. But God is not "on the side of the poor" as much as he is on the side of righteousness and justice.

Prior to the 1960s it was commonly accepted that there are two types of poor people: (1)the "deserving poor" who were victims of misfortune or social injustice; and (2)the "undeserving poor," miscreants who were impoverished due to bad character, bad life choices, unhealthy addictions and self-destructive behavior. By failing to draw a moral distinction between the "deserving" and "undeserving" poor, liberals exempt the latter from moral accountability, and all poverty is attributed to factors outside the individual him/herself – be it "racism," "sexism," or some other form of "social injustice."

When moral categories of "white" and "black" are redefined along racial lines – such as in the case of BLT when "white" becomes synonymous with oppression and "black" with victimhood – the implication is that all white people are by nature privileged oppressors and all blacks (and other minorities) are oppressed victims. In such a scenario the distinctions between individuals dissolves into broad race-based categories that are as simplistic as they are unrealistic.

It is this issue of perpetual victimhood that most concerns Anthony Bradley, a black evangelical scholar who has written extensively on Black Liberation Theology. According to Bradley, BLT is intrinsically counterproductive due to its overemphasis on black victimology. As he writes in his book, *Liberating Black Theology* (2010)...

> The major flaw of black liberation theology is that it views people perpetually as victims....
>
> Black liberation theology was doomed from the beginning because its initial biblical and theological presuppositions were grounded in the reduction of the black experiences in America to that of victim....
>
> Victimology also wove its way through the social ethics of black liberation theologians and set the stage for the adoption of Marxism as an ethical framework for liberation theology....

> Victimology... is perpetuating problems for black America, not solving them. [Anthony Bradley, *Liberating Black Theology: The Bible and the Black Experience in America* (Crossway Books, 2010), p. 14*ff*.]

John McWhorter, a former professor of linguistics at the University of California (Berkeley) and currently a Senior Fellow at the Manhattan Institute, contends that the pathology of black victimology has five very negative consequences: First, Blacks begin to define themselves essentially as victims of white racism to the extent that victimhood becomes the core of their identity. As McWhorter writes in *Losing the Race: Self-Sabotage in Black America* (2001), victimology is "a subconscious, culturally inherited affirmation that life for blacks in America has been... and will be a life of being victimized by the oppression of whites."

Second, black victimology does nothing to solve the very real racial tensions in society – and in fact it actually manufactures them. As McWhorter puts it, "Victimology imagines racism even where there is no evidence." Third, it inhibits self-responsibility. By overemphasizing past discrimination and the current obstacles that blacks still face, victimology provides a cover for all kinds of personal failures and even criminality. Fourth, victimology presents a formidable obstacle to racial reconciliation. He notes that the result is that "the remnants of discrimination hold an obsessive indignant fascination that allows only passing acknowledgment of any signs of progress" and thereby inhibits positive mobility and racial reconciliation.

And finally, the overemphasis on black victimhood plays into socialist ideology. Due to past (and present) injustice, the poor have a right to take from the rich. Socialists tend to equate "social justice" with economic equality, which requires governmental coercion in order to redistribute wealth through confiscatory taxation policies and comprehensive welfare entitlement programs that choke economic investment, productivity and growth, and contribute to massive budget deficits that threaten to eventually bankrupt the nation.

Rev. Jeremiah Wright and Trinity United Church of Christ

For twenty years Barack Obama was a member of Trinity United Church of Christ on the South Side of Chicago, the largest church in the UCC denomination with more than 8,000 members. Originally, the church was founded in 1961 and included mostly affluent blacks. For the first several years Trinity was a generally conventional mainline Protestant church, and like other UCC congregations it followed a standard Protestant order of worship. Church leaders discouraged shouting, hand-waving and other emotional outbursts that were common in many black congregations.

Being situated in a predominantly black and poor area of Chicago, Trinity UCC was actively involved in the civil rights campaigns of the 1960s. By the end of the decade, and especially after the assassination of Martin Luther King Jr., the idealism of the early years began to wane, and as militant Black Power became more influential in the community the church drafted a new mission statement that began with this proclamation:

> We are a congregation which is Unashamedly Black and Unapologetically Christian.... We are an African people, and remain 'true to our native land,' the mother continent, the cradle of civilization. God has superintended our pilgrimage through the days of slavery, the days of segregation, and the long night of racism. It is God who gives us the strength and courage to continuously address injustice as a people, and as a congregation. We constantly affirm our trust in God through cultural expression of a Black worship service and ministries which address the Black Community. [www.trinitychicago.org/index]

With the church's membership in decline, the elders called Rev. Jeremiah Wright (b. 1941) to pastor the church in 1972. Wright grew up in Germantown, a middle-class neighborhood in Philadelphia, where his father served as pastor of Grace Baptist Church for 42 years and his mother was a schoolteacher and administrator. At age fifteen Wright was arrested for grand larceny auto theft, and after high school his parents sent him to all-black Virginia Union University, where he dropped out after two years. (Years later, Wright said that he had hated attending "black schools founded by white missionaries.") Wright joined the US Marine Corps but soon quit and enlisted in the US Navy, where he served for the next four years. Following his discharge he graduated from Howard University and received a master's degree from the University of Chicago Divinity School and a D.Min. from United Theological Seminary in Dayton, Ohio.

When Wright answered the call to pastor Trinity UCC, he was an enthusiastic visionary and an animated apostle of Black Liberation Theology. Reaching out to the surrounding community, he began attracting more poor blacks from Chicago's impoverished South Side. In the process he declared his intention to "recontextualize Christianity" in order to counter the influence of Black Muslims and others who criticized Christianity as "the white man's religion." In the first few years of his ministry some middle-class black families quit the church, accusing Wright of being too strident and militant, but he dismissed them as "Uncle Toms" and "bourgeois Negroes who wanted to be white."

By the time he retired in 2008 Wright had increased Trinity's membership from a hundred people to over 8,000. The congregation, although comprised of mostly poor inner-city blacks, also included many prominent politicians, community leaders and even several celebrities – most notably, Oprah Winfrey. According to a *Newsweek* article in 2008, Winfrey joined the church in the mid-1980s but left in the early '90s because she feared that her association with Rev. Wright might affect her popularity and credibility with her fan base. ["Something Wasn't Wright," *Newsweek* (May 12, 2008).]

Winfrey's concerns were well-considered. Over the years Wright has become famous (or infamous) for his provocative and controversial pulpit rants that have earned him the well-deserved reputation as a bigoted buffoon. According to Wright, Jesus was an "African Jew," as were most of the other figures in the Bible. He has written in *Africans Who Shaped Our Faith* (1995) that "Evidence exists within and outside the Bible to support the notion that the people of Israel... were of African descent," which of course is nonsense. A master of historical revisionism, he also preaches that Jesus was a poor black man who suffered under the oppression of rich whites.

In a particularly provocative sermon on September 16, 2010, "The Day of Jerusalem's Fall," marking the tenth anniversary of the Nine-Eleven attacks, Wright embarked on one of his most notorious tirades when he declared,

> We bombed Hiroshima. We bombed Nagasaki. And we nuked far more than the thousands in New York and the Pentagon – and we never batted an eye!...
>
> We supported state terrorism against the Palestinians and black South Africans and now we are indignant because the stuff we have done overseas is now brought right back into our own front yards. [Cited in Charles C. Johnson, "The Gospel According To Wright." *American Spectator* Dec/Jan 2011).]

Wright closed the sermon by invoking Malcom X's caustic comment on the assassination of JFK: "America's chickens! Coming home to roost!" Furthermore, he added, we shouldn't be praying and singing "God bless America" but rather "God damn America!"

In addition, Wright has been accused of virulent anti-Semitism. In an interview with the *Daily Press of Newport News* on June 9, 2009, a few months into the Obama administration, he indicated that he had not had contact with the President in many months because "Them Jews aren't going to let him talk to me." Under pressure, he later modified his comment and added, "I misspoke. Let me just say: Zionists.... I'm not talking about all Jews... I'm talking about Zionists." But entrenched bigotry is hard to contain, and it wasn't too long afterward that he was quoted as calling the state of Israel "illegal" and "genocidal." [Cited in Wikipedia, "Jeremiah Wright"]

Despite Wright's early comments about "recontextualizing Christianity" in order to counter the influence of Black Muslims and other anti-Christian groups, he evidently reveres Malcolm X, whose birthday is celebrated annually at Trinity UCC. In 1984 Wright accompanied Louis Farrakhan, the acidic racist and anti-Semitic head of the Nation of Islam, on a trip to Libya to confer with Farrakhan's benefactor, the dictator Muammar Gaddafi. Wright also joined Farakhan in 1995 for the Nation of Islam's "Million Man March" in Washington, D.C., and over the years he has boasted of his trips to Castro's Cuba and Daniel Ortega's Communist regime in Nicaragua.

Wright retired in February 2008 after pastoring Trinity UCC for 36 years, whereupon the church bought him a lot in Tinley Park, a predominantly white Chicago suburb, and built a 10,000-square-foot mansion valued at $1.6 million next to the elite Odyssey Country Club. Reportedly, the house features a master bedroom with a whirlpool, an elevator, a butler's pantry, an exercise room, a four-car garage, and a large spare room that can be converted into either an in-home theater or a swimming pool.

Obama Christianity

Barack Obama's exposure to Christianity and his identification with the Christian faith came primarily under the tutelage of Rev. Jeremiah Wright. In addition, Obama has also credited James Cone for having inspired him.

Growing up, Obama had no particular religious affiliation. His father, Barack Obama Sr., was a nominal Muslim from Kenya and a socialist economist who abandoned the family when young Barack was only three-years-old. His mother, Ann Dunham, was by various accounts either an atheist or an agnostic. In his 1995 memoir, *Dreams From My Father*, Obama described her as a

liberal "secular humanist," and he later commented on his lack
of a religious upbringing in his 2006 book, *The Audacity of Hope*:

> I was not raised in a religious household.... My
> mother's own experiences... only reinforced this
> inherited skepticism. Her memories of the Christians
> who populated her youth were not fond ones.... And yet
> for all her professed secularism, my mother was in
> many ways the most spiritually awakened person that
> I've ever known....
>
> [Religion for her was] just one of the many ways –
> and not necessarily the best way – that man attempted
> to control the unknowable and understand the deeper
> truths about our lives. [Cited in Wikipedia, "Ann Dunham."]

Ann Dunham's second husband, Lolo Soetoro, was also a
nominal Muslim but apparently more of a free-floating spiritual
pluralist. The other significant male influence in Obama's life and
a man whom he regarded as a kind of mentor in his adolescent
years was Frank Marshall Davis,* a Communist and a professed
atheist.

Until it became too much of a political liability to acknowledge
it, Obama freely admitted that Rev. Wright had been his spiritual
mentor. He took the title of his second book, *The Audacity of Hope*,
from a sermon that Wright preached in 1990, and Obama and his
wife attended Trinity for twenty years and raised their children in
the church. In 2007 Obama told a group in ministers that Wright
helped "introduce me to my Christian faith," and he later added,

---

* In the opinion of Gerald Horne, an editor of the Communist Party
of the United States of America (CPUSA) publication *Political Affairs*,
Frank Marshall Davis was "a decisive influence in helping Obama to
find his present identity" as an African-American. [Gerald Horne,
"Rethinking the History and Future of the Communist Party," *Political Affairs
Magazine* (March 28, 2007).] Note: This article has been deleted from
the *Political Affairs Magazine* website but is still available at
Archive.org.

"He was like family to me. He strengthened my faith, officiated my wedding, and baptized my children." [Cited in Charles C. Johnson, "The Gospel According To Wright."]

Wright's patronage provided Obama with the street credibility he needed to succeed in community organizing and development and, later, in the tough and competitive world of Chicago politics. Trinity was the largest and most prestigious church on the city's South Side, and Rev. Wright had an impressive record for getting his preferred candidates elected to office. However, as Obama continued his meteoric rise in the Democratic Party and eventually set his sights on the presidency, his long-time association with Jeremiah Wright became a political liability that he could ill afford, as Charles Johnson noted in his article, "The Gospel According to Wright," in the January 2011 issue of *The American Spectator*:

> In 2008 America elected a president whose pastor for 20 years preached anti-Semitic conspiracy theories, advocated bizarre pseudo-scientific racial ideas, opposed interracial marriage, praised communist dictatorships, denounced black "assimilation," and taught Afrocentric feel-good nonsense. [Ibid.]

It wasn't until May 2008, when negative publicity about Jeremiah Wright began to impact his presidential campaign, that Obama resigned his membership from Trinity UCC. Since then, he and his family have rarely attended church even on Christmas and Easter.

A Conclusion

Barack Obama holds positions on a wide range of moral and church/state issues in keeping with a radical secular/liberal agenda. As a result, many Christians find his policies and programs both alarming and repugnant, and many question his sincerity when he professes to be a Christian.

Unless we know someone personally or otherwise have virtually indisputable evidence, we simply are not qualified to judge the spiritual condition of another person's soul. I hope and pray that Barack Obama is a sincere believer in Jesus Christ and that he has experienced a true spiritual conversion, but like many Christians I find many of his values, policies and programs to be inconsistent with biblical principles and teachings.

Perhaps he is indeed sincere, or maybe he is simply an opportunist who has used his identification with the Christian faith to advance his personal ambitions and his political career. One thing is evident, however. His interpretive paradigm for understanding the Christian faith has been shaped primarily by two factors – mainline Protestant liberal theology and Black Liberation Theology – both of which seriously distort the basic tenets of orthodox biblical Christianity.

So when Barack Obama claims that his Christian faith inspired him to pronounce his blessing on same-sex marriage, perhaps he is sincere. Nonetheless, he is wrong – just as he is wrong on many other issues including abortion and the proper relationship between church and state. Sincerity is essential to accessing truth, but it is never sufficient. People are sincerely wrong all the time. What matters is *what* we believe – not how earnestly we believe it – and what matters most is whether our beliefs correspond to God's Truth as revealed in Scripture.

In an age such as ours that has been so polluted by moral and religious relativism, the Bible is an inconvenient reminder that *absolute Truth exists...* and that *it absolutely matters what we believe!* Unfortunately, to this point Barack Obama seems not to have gotten the message. Let us pray, both for his sake and that of our nation, that he gets it soon.

Jefrey Breshears, Ph.D., is a Christian historian, apologist, and the founder and president of The Areopagus, a Christian education ministry and study center in the Atlanta area that offers seminars and forums in Christian history, apologetics, Christian spirituality, and contemporary cultural issues. JBreshears@TheAreopagus.org

Notes and Reflections

....

....

....

....

....

....

....

....

....

....

....

....

....

....

....

....

....

....

....

....

....

....

....

Notes and Reflections

Notes and Reflections

www.ingramcontent.com/pod-product-compliance
Lightning Source LLC
Chambersburg PA
CBHW060631030426
42337CB00018B/3309